TIFFANY

ALL COLOUR PAPERBACKS
Other titles include

Erté
Mucha
Alma Tadema
Burne-Jones
Kate Greenaway
The Orientalists
The Liberty Style
Fashion Illustration
Poiret

Hanging head dragonfly glass shade set with amber glass cabochons, on gilt bronze base.

TIFFANY

A RIZZOLI PAPERBACK

ACKNOWLEDGEMENTS
I should like to thank Minna Rosenblatt Ltd. for supplying transparencies for Plates 18-20, 34, 36, 37 and 39; Alastair Duncan of Christie's, New York for the cover and Plate 35; and Sotheby's, Belgravia for Plate 40 and the frontispiece. Plate 38 is from Editions Graphiques Gallery, London and Plates 9 and 22 are from private collections. All other items are from the Haworth Museum, Accrington and I am particularly grateful to Mr. Potter, the curator, for all his assistance and for allowing us to photograph their collection.

Cover
Leaded glass shade of Snowball design on leaf and arc bronze base.

First published in the United States of America in 1979 by
RIZZOLI INTERNATIONAL PUBLICATIONS, INC.
712 Fifth Avenue/New York 10019

Copyright © 1979 Academy Editions London
All rights reserved
No parts of this book may be
reproduced in any manner whatsoever
without permission in writing from Academy Editions

Library of Congress Catalog Card Number 79-64359
ISBN 0-8478-0234-5

Printed and bound in Hong Kong

INTRODUCTION

Tiffany glass is one of the most beautiful and variegated creations within the Art Nouveau movement. It comes in an extraordinary choice of shapes and colours and in several techniques, many of which are illustrated here. They are the product of an era of sumptuousness, created by a man brought up to expect the best.

Louis Comfort Tiffany was born in 1848, eleven years after his father, Charles Lewis Tiffany, had founded his first New York City store in partnership with his future brother-in-law. Starting out as a small stationery and fancy goods store, its range was soon extended to jewellery, bronzes, watches and clocks. In 1850 the store began to produce its own designs of flatware and other items made in silver of Sterling Standard as set in Great Britain, the first time an American firm had done this for its whole range. The Civil War years proved boom years for Tiffany & Company, the name the firm had taken in 1853 and which it has retained to the present. Charles Tiffany was able to indulge his taste for fine gems and he soon accumulated one of the world's finest collections of gem stones and historic jewellery.

The young Tiffany grew up in an atmosphere of wealth and comfort. Although his father had expected him to eventually take over the management of Tiffany & Co., Louis Comfort Tiffany was determined to forge a career of his own as a painter. While his father did not consider this to be a respectable occupation, he placed no obstacles in Louis' way. After graduating from Flushing Academy, Long Island, at the age of eighteen he was apprenticed to George Inness, a landscape painter, in whose studio he was to remain some two years.

Tiffany first exhibited one of his paintings in 1867 at the National Academy of Design in New York. A year later he left for Paris to study and afterwards travelled in North Africa and Europe. On his return to New York in 1870 Tiffany exhibited in his studio the pictures he had painted during his travels. He exhibited pictures in various American shows throughout the 1870s, displaying a more than competent style, though he was diffident about his difficulties in painting the human figure.

Tiffany & Co. took a stand at the 1878 Paris International Exhibition and was the first American firm to receive an award in Europe for its silverware. That same year they exhibited at the Philadelphia Centennial Exhibition. Louis Comfort Tiffany exhibited some paintings at the family firm's stand, and was very impressed by the example of British handicrafts shown at the Exposition. The New York Society of Decorative Arts was formed to give lectures and classes on these crafts to women and Louis Comfort Tiffany was persuaded to teach there. He soon decided that more than teaching was needed and in 1879 founded Louis C. Tiffany and Associated Artists, with Samuel Colman and Candace Wheeler, aided by Lockwood de Forest - all friends who had been lecturing with him. The new firm set about decorating the homes of the wealthy, many of whom Tiffany had already met through his family firm. In the years that followed he decorated the homes of people such as Cornelius Vanderbilt in New York, Potter Palmer in Chicago and Lily Langtry in London; redecorated a number of rooms at the White House in Washington for President Chester Arthur; and decorated several New York theatres, a yacht and Mark Twain's home. Surrounding himself with the finest craftsmen, of whom he employed about a hundred, he ensured that each decorative scheme was coordinated in style and colours, including the furniture, wallpaper, carpets, light fittings, tapestries and bed-covers. Antiques and *objets d'art* of all kinds were also imported and sold by the firm.

His obsession with the total environment in decoration soon aroused his interest in leaded glass windows. Stained, painted and etched glass irritated him because he felt the process interfered with the full play of light through the glass. He wanted a window to glow like a jewel. He therefore began to experiment with a number of ideas, eventually employing chemists to research various formulae for achieving new colours as well as iridescence and opalescence. Glass workers were employed to experiment with moulding and otherwise treating the glass panes to achieve different finishes. This vast choice of colour and texture thus enabled the window designer to build up the images purely in terms of glass and leading, eschewing painting, staining or etching.

The death of his wife Mary in 1884, after twelve years of marriage, left him in great distress. He had split with Associated Artists two years earlier and although he had retained his decorating firm under the name Louis C. Tiffany & Co., this was going through some business difficulties. The Madison Square Theatre, which he had just decorated, had had several failed productions and the owners were unable to meet his bills. He sued the theatre, forced its public sale and bought it himself. He was to own it until the new manager was able to buy it from him. In the meantime he had thrown himself into New York night life. This rather worried his father, who commissioned him to decorate a new and large family mansion on Madison Avenue and 72nd Street. Charles Tiffany never lived in it, though Louis Comfort Tiffany retained the use of the top floor studio and flat for his own use, and one is tempted to think that the father thought of this mansion as therapy for the son. In 1886 Louis Comfort Tiffany married Louise Wakeman Knox, a clergyman's daughter. He expanded the business, carrying out a number of commissions from architects, and executed a vast number of windows for various churches, many of which were subsequently destroyed along with the churches.

Although Tiffany had founded the Tiffany Glass Company in 1885, this was still entirely devoted to executing interior designs and the making and assembling of cathedral glass for leaded windows, most of the glass itself still being made in other glasshouses. Four years later, however, he accompanied Edward C. Moore, his father's colleague and chief designer, to the 1889 International Exhibition in Paris. There he saw for the first time the full range of the new glass being produced by European designers: inventive crackled glass by Leveillé, original designs by Gallé, formal cameo carved vessels from the various English Stourbridge firms, hardstone effects achieved by Loetz and early iridescent glass vessels by Lobmeyr, Pantin and Webb. He also met Samuel Bing, a leading Paris dealer in works of art from the Far East.

Bing toured the United States in 1892 carrying out a survey of American art and industry on behalf of the French Government. Tiffany, who had just formed the Tiffany Glass and Decorating Company to manufacture and market glass and other decorative objects and materials, was Bing's host. Bing persuaded Tiffany to design and manufacture a complete chapel with all its furniture and fittings for display at the Chicago Columbian World's Fair. This proved extremely successful and won Tiffany fifty-four medals. Their association continued when Bing commissioned Tiffany to execute a series of leaded glass windows after designs by a number of Paris artists, including Toulouse-Lautrec, Bonnard, Grasset, Vallotton and Vuillard. Later, in 1895 Bing transformed his shop in Paris into a gallery called L'Art Nouveau, where he displayed all that was most striking in the new arts and crafts.

In 1892 Tiffany met Arthur J. Nash, an Englishman from Stourbridge, who managed one of the Webb subsidiary glass works there. Although he was touring the United States to promote his firm's wares, Tiffany persuaded him to join him in founding a new glassworks in New York. The Stourbridge Glass Company was incorporated in April 1893 with a factory at Corona, Long Island. Shortly after the opening, however, the factory burned down. Tiffany rebuilt it and although Nash remained as Vice-President under Tiffany's Presidency, he had to accept that he could not be considered a full partner in the firm. Nash hired a number of glassworkers from the Boston and Sandwich Glass Company, which had just gone out of business after a prolonged strike, and brought over a number of other workers from England. The works quickly expanded and were constituted into one glass shop devoted to the manufacture of cathedral glass for use in leaded windows, and an experimental shop in which new techniques, designs and models were tried out. Other shops opened as needed, and there was a laboratory where several chemists worked on experimental formulae for achieving various effects. Later, a foundry and metal shop were set up.

The first glass produced at Corona included laminated glass in imitation of cut agate, which was somewhat similar to the glass exhibited by Loetz at the 1889 Paris Fair. It proved more difficult to obtain an iridescent finish on glass vessels than on flat sheets as used in leaded windows, but Tiffany's chemists persevered and he was soon producing an extraordinary range of lustred effects. Much of the first year's production went to various museums, while a batch of it was sent to Bing's gallery in Paris.

Tiffany glass was soon being produced in a wide range of styles, designs and techniques. Tiffany himself designed a number of shapes, frequently explaining his intentions or else bringing items from his collection of ancient glass to be copied, this task to be carried out by the chemists, technicians and glass workers. He retained control over his products, as well as maintaining exclusiveness, by retailing only through a select number of luxury stores in addition to Tiffany & Company in New York and London, Bing's L'Art Nouveau in Paris and his own Tiffany Studios. His glass was not sold to these outlets, but only sent to them on consignment. Items unsold after three months were returned to the factory and sent to another outlet. Items still unsold after being sent to three consignees were normally smashed on their return. Tiffany also had his representatives tour all accessible second-hand shops to buy back any of his glass which might turn up there.

Within a short while two of Tiffany's products became the hallmark of a smart and fashionable environment. No home was complete without some Tiffany glass and at least one Tiffany lamp. While the earliest lamps were made in blown glass, the most popular were those with leaded glass shades set on a bronze base. The shades themselves were made in hundreds of different patterns and colours, many of them with floral designs, others with dragonflies, spiderwebs or abstract shapes. The bases were originally designed to contain oil, but the advent of electricity allowed a number of new shapes to develop. Although the bases were generally made of bronze, some were also covered in mosaics or made of pottery.

Another venture of Tiffany's was a glass mosaics shop headed by Joseph Briggs, another Englishman A number of mosaic panels were executed, including a vast design by Maxfield Parish for the Curtis Publishing Company in Philadelphia, and a mosaic curtain for the National Theatre in Mexico City.

Success for Tiffany's glass meant awards, medals and the French Legion of Honour for him at the 1900 Paris Universal Exhibition, as well as a vast number of other awards at every major exhibition in which he participated. After his father's death in 1902 Tiffany became Vice-President and artistic director of Tiffany & Co. He essayed a number of new crafts, including jewellery and pottery, and bought himself an estate at Oyster Bay, Long Island, where he built an enormous house which he hoped to turn into a memorial of his life and work. Dedicated to the pursuit of the ideal of beauty throughout his life, his intense activity and production was slowed by the outbreak of war in Europe in 1914, in which the United States was to join in 1916. Many of Tiffany's workers joined the army or went into war work. When war ended in 1918 Tiffany was seventy years old. He set up the Louis Comfort Tiffany Foundation to aid promising young artists, giving it eighty acres of his estate, including his house, the art gallery and his art collection, later also giving it most of the shares he held in his company. In 1920 he and Nash retired. The company was split into two separate compartments, Louis C. Tiffany Furnaces Inc., under the control of Nash's son, A. Douglas Nash, who continued the production of a wide variety of glass and other goods; and Tiffany Studios, run by Joseph Briggs, which remained as a retail organisation selling its vast stock of glass and other goods, though leaded glass shades went on being assembled for many years from stock glass sheets.

Tiffany lived to see his popularity wane, his products derided and ridiculed, the students at his Foundation working in styles he had no sympathy for. He objected to the commercialisation of his name by A. Douglas Nash and withdrew his financial support in 1928, when the factory was closed down and its stocks given to Tiffany Studios. Young Nash purchased the glassworks from Tiffany and tried to carry on there on his own, but eventually closed down. Tiffany died in 1933, shortly before his eighty-fifth birthday. That same year Joseph Briggs visited his native Accrington. He brought his collection with him and gave half of it to the town and the other half to his family, several members of whom later donated items to the town collection, now housed at the Haworth Art Gallery. He kept Tiffany Studios going until his death in 1936. Two years later the rest of the Studios stock was sold at auction. After the Second World War the Tiffany Foundation sold off the Tiffany collection and the house and estate to provide additional scholarships. The house later burned down. A few years later the Tiffany revival was in full swing.

Victor Arwas

1

Left: Decorated Favrile glass perfume bottle and stopper.
Right: Agate vase. The laminated effect was produced by mixing molten glass in a number of opaque colours at a temperature low enough to prevent their fusing. On cooling, various layers, or strata, were found. The vessel was then polished or cut into facets which displayed a remarkable resemblance to agate in the internal patterns and colours.

2

A sample cut of Millefiore glass showing flowers made by inserting grouped glass canes of various colours into the parison, smoothing it on the marver, then cutting across to show sections of the canes, which form various floral or cog-wheel shapes.

3

Section of mosaic design using iridescent Favrile glass tesserae.

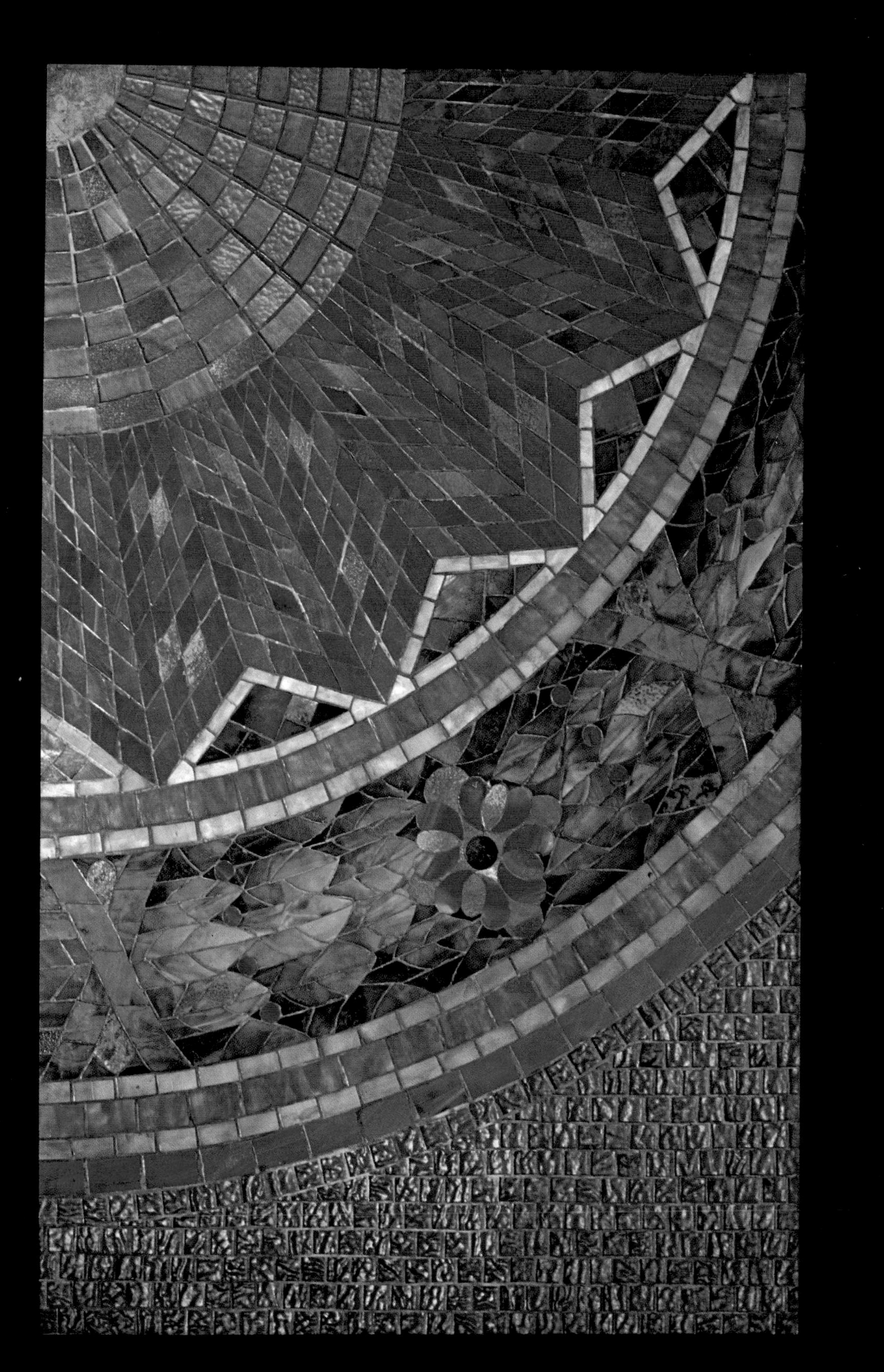

4

Gold vase with a bulging neck over a strangulated waist, the effect being almost that of two vases fused together.

5

Peacock vase. First introduced in 1895, this pattern was made using a mixture of five different types of glass, the feather effect being achieved by combing. The feather 'eyes' were then inserted into the parison and smoothed.

6

Jack-in-the Pulpit vase. One of Tiffany's most successful Art Nouveau designs, this flower form depended for its gracefulness on the contrast between the sweeping elongated fine stem and the wide pinched, curly corolla. It was made in iridescent gold and blue glass in two basic sizes.

8

Iridescent vase with an overall pattern of large heart-shaped leaves and vines.

9

Massive iridescent dark blue vase with silver lustred leaf and vine pattern.

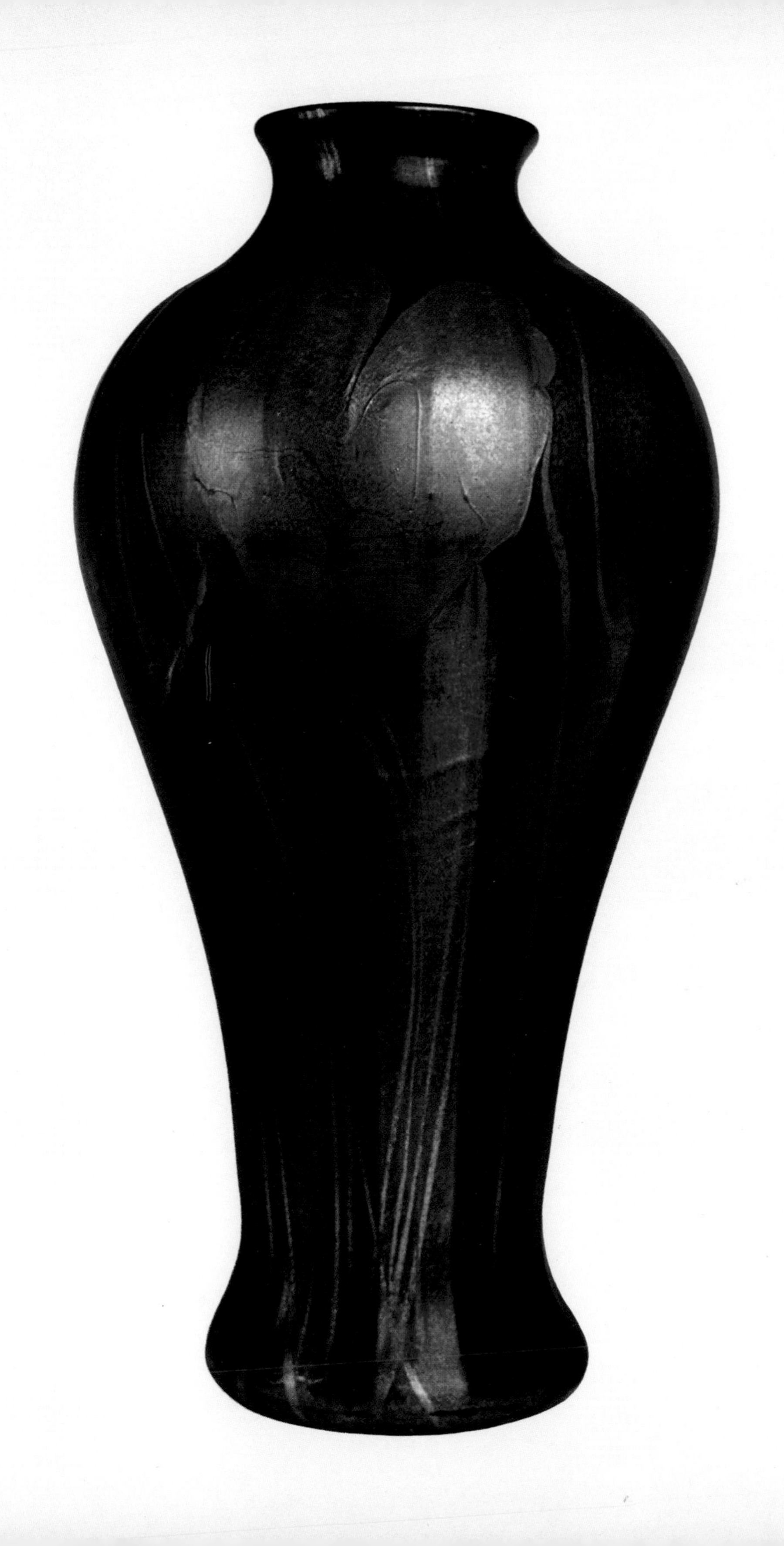

10

Tel El Amarna vase, named after the site of the excavations in Egypt of the Pharaoh Amenhotep IV's capital. Tiffany had visited the site, which inspired a series of often large vases of simple symmetrical shapes with a spectacular matt lustred surface, generally in a rich blue colour, but sometimes executed in red or ochre. They generally have gold iridescent rings and are decorated with one or more chain-pattern bands in clearly defined areas.

11

Iridescent gold vase, the pinched design creating deep crevasses in which light can reveal reflections in a variety of colours.

12

Cypriote vase. Created in imitation of the natural decay of ancient glass buried in the sand for centuries, these vases were made by rolling the blown vessel over a layer of crushed glass of the same type on the marver, then lustring it. Always made in simple, uncluttered shapes, their surfaces are pitted all over, frequently with exploded bubbles. They are often decorated with abstract or wavy patterns.

13

Bulbous shaped Cypriote vase. The surface-exploded bubbles are clearly visible, a miniature lunar landscape.

14

Lava vase. The open mouth of the vase shows its highly lustred interior.

16

Vase with highly lustred surface broken up into blues and greens.

17

Black glass vase with lustred gold scroll pattern decoration.

18

Black glass vase decorated with an overall silver lustre pattern.

19

Rosewater sprinkler vase, the green glass decorated with pulled lustred glass threads.

20

Flower-form vase in lustred glass with pulled thread decoration, the flower head bowl joined to the circular base by a long slender stem. All the Tiffany flower-form vases were free blown.

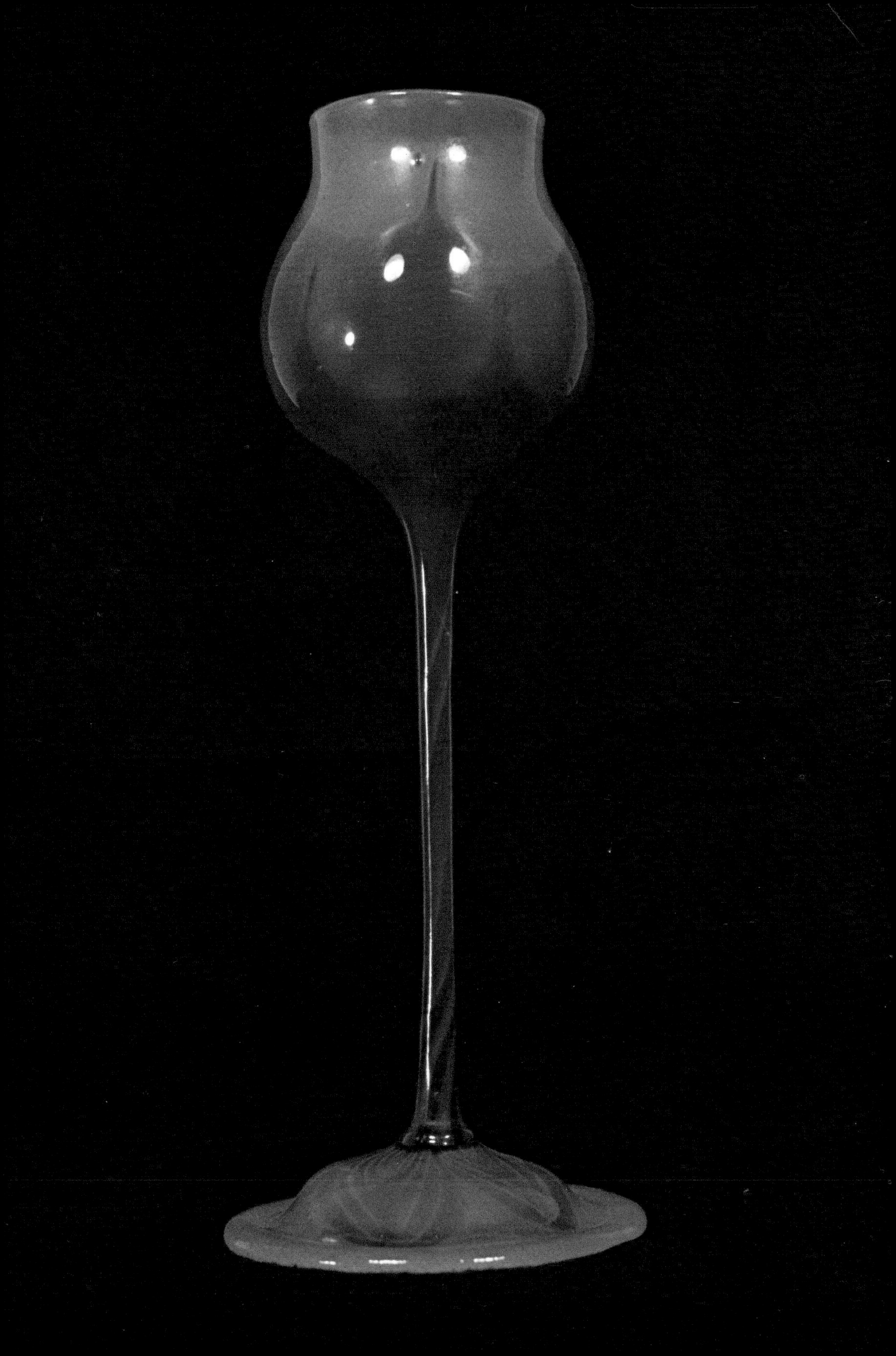

21

Leaf and Vine vase. This was one of the most popular Tiffany designs and was made in a wide variety of colour combinations.

22

Goose-neck vase of Persian rosewater flask design decorated with peacock feathers in silver lustre.

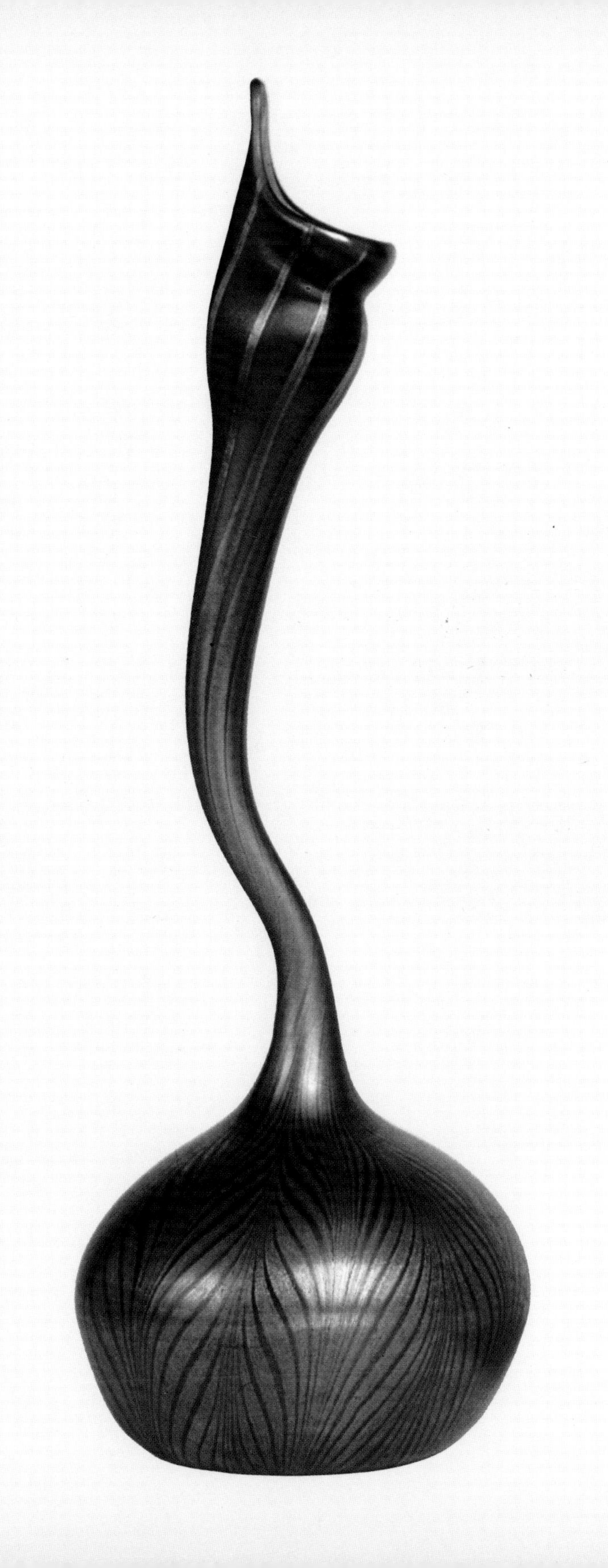

23

Two vases in clear glass padded with blobs of coloured glass, carved in cameo and intaglio with designs of plants and fruit.

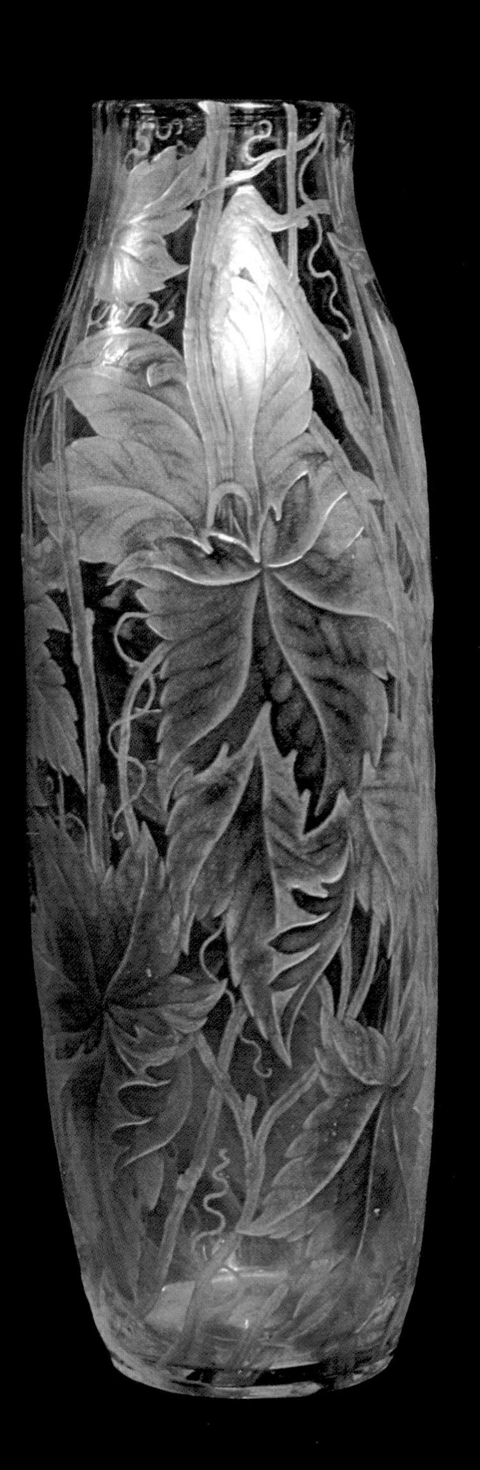
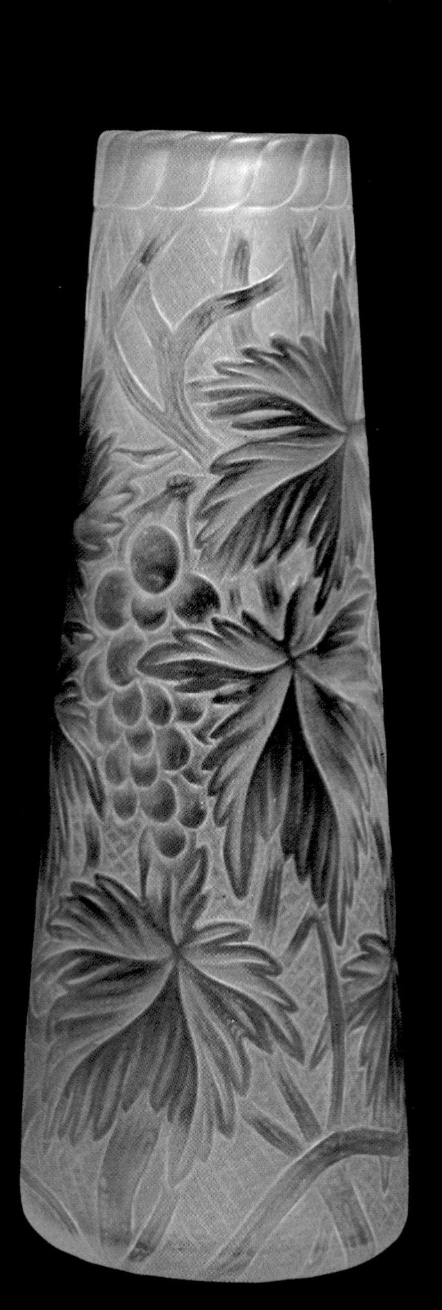

24

Transparent vase padded with blobs of green glass, the green glass cameo carved as leaves, the clear glass intaglio carved with an intricate pattern of stems.

25

Cased opaque vase, cameo-carved with yellow blossoms.

26

Cased vase in opal, yellow and amber glass, intaglio-carved in a lattice chain pattern on the outer surface and lustred.

27

Paperweight vase with embedded millefiore flowers.

28

Paperweight vase in which the inner layer of transparent glass is decorated, here with a leaf design, then encased in an outer layer of transparent glass. The inner surface of paperweight vases was frequently lustred.

29

Reactive paperweight vase. Here reactive glass was used in the decoration of the inner layer and this changed colour and became iridescent when reheated.

31

Cased vase with tiny pulled handles, the rare red outer surface polished to a high gloss.

32

Iridescent Favrile glass tiles. These were used in various decorative schemes for fireplaces, fountains, table-tops, etc. Individual tiles were occasionally bronze-mounted as trivets.

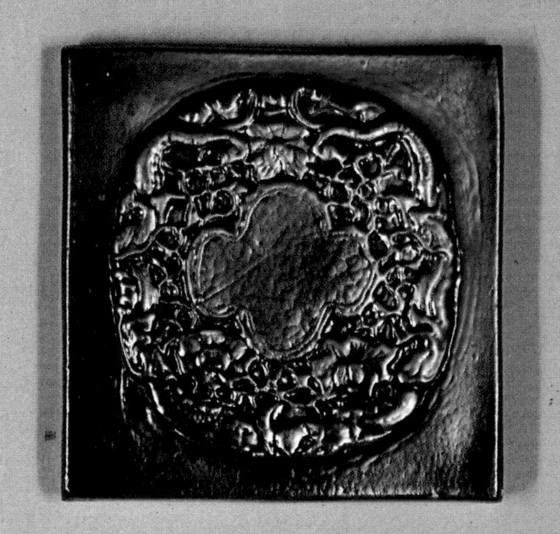
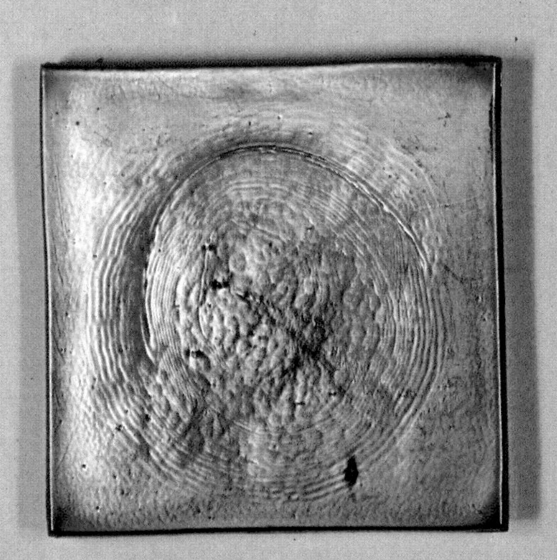

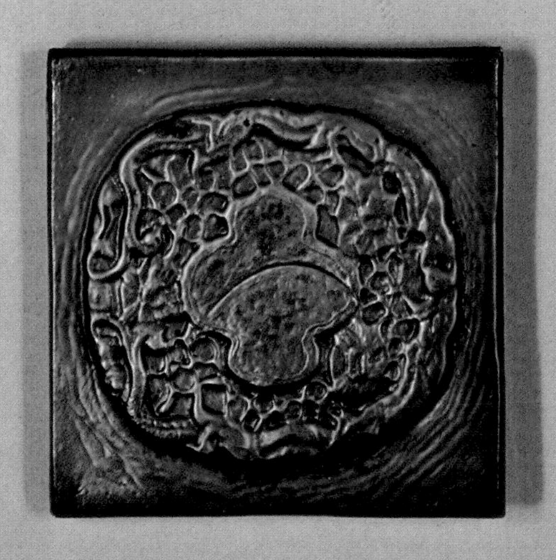

33

Turtleback tiles in iridescent Favrile glass. In the manufacture of lamps these were often used on shades as well as bases.

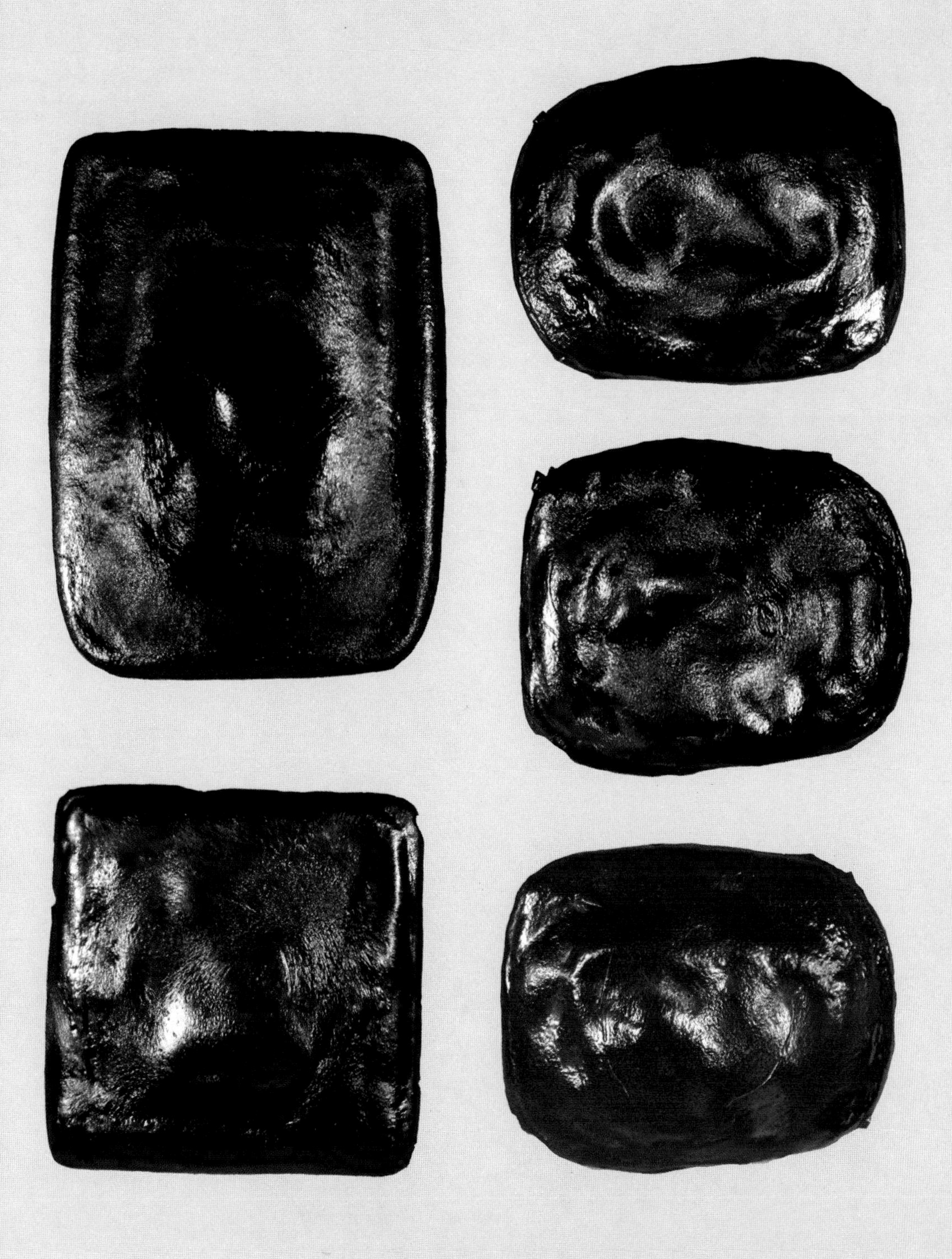

34

Two stemmed wine glasses in lustred pastel coloured glass.

35

Spiderweb leaded glass shade over a bronze oil can base with wheatstalks and leaves on a mosaic of glass tesserae.

37

Leaded glass shade of Oriental Poppy design on bronze base.

38

Leaded glass shade of Apple Blossom design on bronze base.

39

Leaded glass shade of Daffodil design on bronze base.